Table of Contents

Introduction

Miniature pies are all the rage today! What is there not to like about miniature pies? The tiny bite sized pies are not only easy to eat, but they are just as easy to prepare as well. These kinds of pies are completely customizable, meaning that you can make pies that are not only packed with a sweet flavor, but that are savory and filling as well. Whether you want to make a sweet dessert for the upcoming holidays season or whether you want something savory to serve for dinner, you have certainly come to the right place.

Throughout this cookbook, you will discover how to prepare the most delicious and simplest miniature pies that you can make from the comfort of your own home. By the end of this cookbook, it is my hope that you will not only have access to over 25 miniature pie recipes that you can prepare, but that you find new and exciting dishes to serve to your family.

So, let's stop wasting time and get to baking some miniature pies!

Miniature Raspberry Pies

These miniature pies are perfect for entertaining your guests during your next lunch or dinner event. They are easy to make and absolutely adorable.

Makes: 36 servings

Total Prep Time: 1 hour and 50 minutes

Ingredients:

- 2 pounds of Fuji apples, peeled and cut into small pieces
- 3 Tbsp. of butter, melted and extra for greasing
- ½ cups of all-purpose flour
- 1 Tbsp. of cornstarch + 1 ½ tsp. of water, mixed together
- ¼ tsp. of salt
- ½ tsp. of powdered cinnamon
- ½ cup of white sugar, evenly divided
- ¼ cup of light brown sugar
- 1 ½ cups of raspberries, sliced into halves and evenly divided
- 1 premade pie crust, cut into 3 rounds

Directions:

1. In a pot set over low to medium heat, add in the apple pieces, raspberries, powdered cinnamon and dash of salt. Cover and cook for 15 minutes or until the apples are soft.
2. Add in the cornstarch mix. Stir well to incorporate. Cook for 3 to 4 minutes or until thick in consistency. Remove from heat and set aside to cool completely.
3. Add in ½ cup of the raspberry halves. Stir well to incorporate.
4. Grease the cups of a miniature muffin pan and add the pie dough rounds into the wells. Cover and place into the fridge to chill for 30 minutes.
5. Preheat the oven to 400 degrees.
6. In a bowl, add in the all-purpose flour, white sugar, dash of salt and 3 tablespoons of melted butter. Stir well until crumbly in consistency.
7. Pour the apple mix into the muffin cups. Sprinkle the crumble over the top.
8. Place into the oven to bake for 20 minutes. Rotate the muffin pan and continue to bake for an additional 10 minutes. Remove and set aside to cool for 5 minutes.
9. Serve immediately.

Miniature Lemon and Butter Pies

This is a delicious pie dish you can make that I know you won't be able to get enough of. It is filled with a unique flavor I know you will love.

Makes: 12 servings

Total Prep Time: 40 minutes

Ingredients:

- ½ cup of butter
- 2 tsp. of grated lemon zest
- 1/3 cup of lemon juice
- 1 ½ cups of white sugar
- 3 eggs
- 2 egg yolks
- 12, 3 inch miniature tart shells, premade
- 3 egg whites
- ¼ cup of white sugar

Directions:

1. In a saucepan set over low to medium heat, add in the butter. Once melted, add in the grated lemon zest, lemon juice and 1 ½ cups of white sugar. Stir well to mix.

2. In a separate bowl, add in the eggs and egg yolks. Whisk until thick in consistency. Add into the lemon mix. Continue to cook for 3 to 4 minutes or until thick in consistency.
3. In a bowl, add in the egg whites. Beat with an electric mixer until the peaks are stiff. Add in ¼ cup of white sugar. Continue to beat until the peaks become glossy.
4. Pour the custard into the tart shells. Top off with the egg white mix.
5. Place into the oven to bake for 25 to 30 minutes at 350 degrees or until golden.
6. Remove and cool for 15 minutes before serving.

Miniature Apple Pies

If there is a delicious pie dish that is perfect to make during the fall season. It is so delicious, I know you will insist on making these miniature pies every chance you get.

Makes: 12 servings

Total Prep Time: 55 minutes

Ingredients:

- 2 store-bought pie crusts
- 2 ½ cups of apples, peeled and chopped
- ¼ cup of white sugar
- 2 Tbsp. of all-purpose flour
- 1 tsp. of powdered cinnamon
- 1 tsp. of pure vanilla
- 1/8 tsp. of powdered nutmeg

Directions:

1. Preheat the oven to 425 degrees.
2. Roll out the pie crusts in 1/8 inch thickness. Use a 3 ½ inch cookie

cutter and cut out 12 circles from the crust. Transfer the dough circles into a greased muffin pan, pressing along the bottom and sides of the cups evenly.

3. In a bowl, add in the chopped apples, white sugar, all-purpose flour, powdered cinnamon, pure vanilla and powdered nutmeg. Stir well until mixed. Pour into the muffin cups.

4. Cover the filling with the remaining pie dough circles.

5. Place into the oven to bake for 20 to 25 minutes at 425 degrees or until golden. Remove and set aside to cool for 10 to 15 minutes.

6. Serve.

Miniature Coconut Cream Pies

These miniature pies are packed with all of the traditional flavors of coconut cream pie that every person will fall in love with.

 Makes: 30 servings

Total Prep Time: 1 hour and 35 minutes

Ingredients for the filling:

- 30 premade miniature phyllo cups
- ¾ cup of coconut milk
- ½ cup of whole milk
- 1/3 cup of white sugar
- ¼ cup of coconut, shredded
- Dash of salt
- 3 egg yolks
- 1 ½ Tbsp. of cornstarch

- 1 Tbsp. of butter, cut into pieces
- ½ tsp. of pure vanilla

Ingredients for the topping:

- ¾ cup of heavy whipping cream
- 1 Tbsp. of white sugar
- 1 tsp. of rum
- ¼ tsp. of pure vanilla
- Coconut, toasted, shredded and for garnish

Directions:

1. In a saucepan set over medium heat, add in the coconut milk, whole milk, half of the white sugar, shredded coconut and dash of salt. Stir to mix and allow to come to a simmer.
2. In a separate bowl, add in the egg yolks, the remaining white sugar and cornstarch. Whisk until smooth in consistency. Add this mix slowly into the saucepan and whisk well to mix. Cook for 1 minute or until thick in consistency.
3. Add in the butter cubes and pure vanilla. Whisk until smooth. Remove from heat and transfer into a bowl. Cover with a sheet of plastic wrap and place into the fridge to chill for 1 hour.
4. Prepare the topping. In the bowl of a stand mixer, add in the heavy whipping cream, white sugar, rum and pure vanilla. Beat on the highest setting until peaks begin to form.
5. Add 1 tablespoon of the coconut cream mix into the phyllo cups. Pipe the whipped cream over the top of the cups.
6. Garnish the pies with shredded coconut
7. Serve immediately.

Cranberry Nut Pies

This is a traditional twist on a nutty classic. These pies are baked to utter perfection in a miniature muffin pan and perfect for the holidays.

 Makes: 24 servings

Total Prep Time: 45 minutes

Ingredients:

- ½ cup of butter, soft
- 1, 3 ounce pack of cream cheese, soft
- 1 cup of all-purpose flour
- 1 egg
- ¾ cup of light brown sugar
- 1 Tbsp. of butter, melted
- 1 tsp. of pure vanilla
- 3 Tbsp. of walnuts, chopped

- 3 Tbsp. of cranberries, chopped

Directions:

1. In a bowl, add in the butter and cream cheese. Stir well to mix. Add in the all-purpose flour and stir well until evenly blended. Cover and set into the fridge to chill for 1 hour.
2. Prepare the filling. In a bowl, add in the egg, light brown sugar, melted butter and pure vanilla. Stir well until mixed. Add in the cranberries and chopped walnuts. Stir well to incorporate.
3. Preheat the oven to 325 degrees.
4. Divide the dough into 1 inch balls. Press into the miniature muffin pans. Spread evenly throughout the bottom and sides.
5. Fill the muffin cups with the filling.
6. Place into the oven to bake for 25 to 30 minutes or until light brown.
7. Remove and cool for 10 minutes before serving.

Miniature Pumpkin Pies

This is the perfect pie dish for you to prepare whenever you want to make several desserts for your next dinner party. One bite and everybody who tries it will become hooked.

 Makes: 24 servings

Total Prep Time: 1 hour

Ingredients:

- 2 premade pie crusts
- 3 eggs, evenly divided
- 1, 8 ounce pack of cream cheese, soft
- ½ cup of white sugar
- 1 cup of pumpkin, canned
- 1 tsp. of pure vanilla
- 1 tsp. of pumpkin pie spice

Directions:

1. Preheat the oven to 350 degrees.
2. Roll out the pie crusts into a rectangle that is 11 inches in size. Cut out 12, 3 inch sized rounds from the dough and transfer into a greased muffin pan.
3. In a bowl, add in one egg white. Whisk until frothy. Brush the

edges of the pie crusts.

4. In a separate bowl, add in one egg yolk and remaining two eggs. Add in the cream cheese, white sugar, canned pumpkin, pure vanilla and pumpkin pie spice. Stir well until smooth in consistency. Pour 2 tablespoons of the mix into each crust.
5. Place into the oven to bake for 15 minutes or until the crusts are golden.
6. Remove and cool for 15 minutes before serving.

Lemon and Honey Butter Pies

This is a natural sweet pie dish that you don't have to feel guilty about enjoying. They are incredibly easy to make and will get plenty of rave reviews.

Makes: 9 servings

Total Prep Time: 40 minutes

Ingredients:

- 2 eggs
- ½ cup of light brown sugar
- ½ cup of honey
- 2 Tbsp. of lemon juice
- 1 tsp. of grated lemon zest
- ½ tsp. of powdered cinnamon
- ¼ tsp. of powdered nutmeg
- ¼ tsp. of salt
- 1/3 cup of butter, melted
- 18, 2 inch miniature pie shells

Directions:

1. Preheat the oven to 375 degrees.
2. In a bowl, add in the eggs. Whisk until lightly beaten. Add in the light brown sugar, honey, lemon juice, grated lemon zest, powdered cinnamon, powdered nutmeg and dash of salt. Stir well to mix.
3. Add in the melted butter and stir well to incorporate.
4. Pour the filling into the miniature pie shells. Transfer onto a baking sheet.
5. Place into the oven to bake for 15 to 20 minutes or until the crusts are golden.
6. Remove and cool for 15 minutes before serving.

Miniature S'mores Pies

Traditional s'mores are typically messy to prepare. However, these delicious miniature s'mores pies are less messy to make and can be ready in just a matter of minutes.

Makes: 12 servings

Total Prep Time: 20 minutes

Ingredients for the crusts:

- 1 ½ cups of graham crackers, crumbled
- 4 Tbsp. of butter, melted
- 1 egg, beaten

Ingredients for the filling:

- ¾ cup of heavy whipping cream
- 8 ounces of semi-sweet chocolate, chopped
- Chocolate shavings, for sprinkling

Ingredients for the topping:

- 2 tsp. of powdered gelatin
- ½ cup of water
- 1 cup of white sugar
- 1/8 tsp. of cream of tartar
- ½ tsp. of pure vanilla
- 1/8 tsp. of salt

Directions:

1. Preheat the oven to 300 degrees. Grease a muffin pan.
2. Prepare the crusts. In a bowl, add in the graham cracker crumbs, melted butter and egg. Stir well to evenly mixed. Press into the greased muffin cups.
3. Place into the oven to bake for 10 minutes. Remove and set aside to cool completely.
4. Prepare the filling. Place the shells of the pie crusts onto a baking sheet. In a saucepan set over low to medium heat, add in the heavy whipping cream. Allow to come to a simmer. Add in the semi-sweet chocolate and stir well until smooth in consistency. Pour into the pie crust shells.
5. Prepare the topping. In the bowl of a stand mixer, add in the gelatin and 2 ounces of water. Whisk to mix.
6. In a saucepan set over medium heat, add in 2 ounces of water, white sugar and cream of tartar. Stir well to evenly mixed. Cook until it reaches a temperature of 240 degrees. Remove from heat and pour into the bowl with the gelatin mix. Add in the pure vanilla and dash of salt. Beat on the highest setting until thick in consistency.
7. Drop the marshmallow mix by the dollops into the pie crusts.
8. Sprinkle the chocolate shavings over the top.
9. Set aside to cool completely before serving.

Miniature Caramel and Cookie Pies

This is a great tasting miniature pie recipe that is wonderful to make for parties. It is made with a sweet and creamy frosting everybody will rave about.

Makes: 48 servings

Total Prep Time: 2 hours and 10 minutes

Ingredients:

- 48, 3 inch miniature pie shells, baked
- 1, 14 ounce pack of caramel candies
- 3 Tbsp. of coffee liqueur
- ½ cup of evaporated milk
- ¼ cup of shortening
- 1 cup of white sugar

- ½ tsp. of pure vanilla
- ½ cup of butter, soft
- 1/3 cup of evaporated milk

Directions:

1. In a double boiler set over medium heat, add in the caramel candies, coffee liqueur and ½ cup of evaporated milk. Stir well to mix. Cook for 2 to 3 minutes or until smooth in consistency. Remove from heat and pour over the miniature pie shells.
2. In a bowl, add in the shortening, white sugar, pure vanilla, butter and remaining evaporated milk. Beat with an electric mixer until smooth in consistency. Pour into the pie shells.
3. Cover and set into the fridge to chill for 2 hours.
4. Remove and serve.

Miniature Lemon Meringue Pies

If you want to show off your baking skills, then this is the perfect dish for you to prepare. They are incredibly simple to make and taste absolutely delicious.

 Makes: 6 servings

Total Prep Time: 1 hour

Ingredients:

- 3 eggs, separated
- ¾ cup of white sugar
- 2 Tbsp. of cornstarch
- 2 Tbsp. of all-purpose flour
- 1 cup of water
- 6 Tbsp. of lemon juice
- 3 Tbsp. of grated lemon zest
- 1 Tbsp. of butter
- 6 miniature graham cracker pie crusts
- ¼ cup of white sugar
- ¼ tsp. of almond extract

Directions:

1. Preheat the oven to 350 degrees.
2. In a bowl, add in three egg yolks. Beat with a whisk until smooth in consistency. Set this mix aside.
3. In a saucepan set over medium heat, add in ¾ cup of white sugar, cornstarch and all-purpose flour. Add in the water, lemon juice and grated lemon zest. Allow to come to a boil. Lower the heat to low. Add in the egg yolks and butter. Whisk until smooth in consistency.
4. Pour the lemon filling into the miniature pie crusts.
5. In a bowl, add in the egg whites, ¼ cup of white sugar and almond extract. Beat with an electric mixer until stiff peaks form. Dollop over the top of the filling.
6. Place into the oven to bake for 10 minutes or until golden.
7. Remove and set aside to cool completely before serving.

Miniature Strawberry Rhubarb Pies

These delicious pies are the perfect balance of delicious fall and winter flavors that is perfect to enjoy just as the weather begins to turn cold.

Makes: 12 servings

Total Prep Time: 1 hour

Ingredients:

- 1 ½ cups of pretzels, crushed
- ¾ cup of butter, melted
- ½ cup of walnuts, crushed
- ¼ cup of light brown sugar
- 2 Tbsp. of maple syrup
- Dash of powdered cinnamon
- Dash of powdered cardamom
- 2 egg whites
- 1 cup of raw sugar
- 2 Tbsp. of self-rising flour
- 1 tsp. of pure vanilla
- ¾ pound of rhubarb, chopped
- 2 cups of strawberries, chopped

Directions:

1. Preheat the oven to 350 degrees. Grease a muffin pan with cooking

spray.

2. In a bowl, add in the crushed pretzels, melted butter, crushed walnuts, light brown sugar, maple syrup, powdered cinnamon and powdered cardamom. Stir well to evenly mix. Pour into the bottom of the muffin cups.
3. In a bowl, add in the egg whites. Beat with an electric mixer until frothy. Add in the raw sugar, flour and pure vanilla. Continue to beat until smooth in consistency.
4. Add in the chopped rhubarb and chopped strawberries. Fold gently to incorporate. Pour into the pie crusts.
5. Place the pie crusts onto a baking sheet.
6. Place into the oven to bake for 30 minutes or until golden on top. Remove and set aside to cool for 10 to 15 minutes.
7. Remove and serve while warm.

Miniature Cherry Pies

These cherry pies are a staple during many family holiday celebrations. They are incredibly tasty and the perfect size for everybody to have their own pie to themselves.

 Makes: 2 servings

Total Prep Time: 1 hour and 15 minutes

Ingredients:

- 1 premade pie crust
- 1, 15 ounce can of sour cherries, pitted and drained
- 2 Tbsp. of quick cooking tapioca
- ½ cup of white sugar
- 1/8 tsp. of almond extract

Directions:

1. Preheat the oven to 400 degrees.
2. Roll out the pie crust and cut out 2, 5 inch sized crusts from the dough. Slice the remaining dough into strips that are 1/8 inch in thickness.
3. In a bowl, add in the cherries, tapioca, white sugar and almond extract. Stir well to mix. Set aside to rest for 5 minutes. Stir and pour into the pie crusts.
4. Add half of the dough strips over the filling vertically. Place the remaining pie crusts over the top horizontally.
5. Place into the oven to bake for 30 minutes or until the crusts are golden.

6. Remove and set aside to cool completely before serving.

Miniature Banana Split Pies

These beautiful and delicious miniature dessert pies are made with a savory graham cracker crust and topped off with a cream cheese filling that will remind you of your favorite banana split dessert.

Makes: 18 servings

Total Prep Time: 1 hour and 15 minutes

Ingredients:

- 2 cups of heavy whipping cream
- 18 miniature graham cracker pie crusts
- ¾ cup of powdered sugar
- 2 Tbsp. of pure vanilla
- 1, 8 ounce pack of cream cheese, soft
- 1, 8 ounce container of whipped topping
- 5 bananas, thinly sliced
- 2, 15 ounce cans of pineapple, crushed and drained
- 1, 16 ounce can of cherry pie filling
- ½ cup of pecans, chopped
- 6 Tbsp. of chocolate syrup

Directions:

1. Preheat the oven to broil at 450 degrees.
2. In a bowl, add in the heavy whipping cream. Beat with an electric mixer until peaks form on the surface. Add in the powdered sugar

and pure vanilla. Continue to beat until the peaks become stiff. Transfer into a piping bag and set into the fridge to chill until ready for use.
3. Place the pie crusts onto a baking sheet. Place into the oven to broil for 3 to 5 minutes or until browned. Remove and set aside to cool.
4. In a separate bowl, add in the cream cheese. Beat with an electric mixer until creamy in consistency. Add in the whipped topping. Fold gently to incorporate. Pour into each of the pie crusts, filling each of the crusts halfway.
5. Place the banana slices over the filling. Spread the crushed pineapples over the top followed by the cherry pie filling.
6. Pipe the whipped cream over the top.
7. Drizzle the chocolate syrup over the whipped cream and a sprinkling of the chopped pecans.
8. Cover and set into the fridge to chill for 30 minutes.
9. Remove and serve.

Miniature English Butter Pies

This is a new and delicious new pie recipe you can make whenever you want to try something new. They are so delicious, I guarantee you will want to make them as often as possible.

Makes: 12 servings

Total Prep Time: 35 minutes

Ingredients:

- 12, 12 inch tart shells
- ½ cup of light brown sugar
- ½ cup of light corn syrup
- ¼ cup of shortening
- 1 egg
- 1 tsp. of pure vanilla
- ¼ tsp. of salt
- ¾ cup of raisins

Directions:

1. Preheat the oven to 400 degrees.
2. Place the tart shells onto a baking sheet. Add the raisins into the bottom of each tart shell. 3. In a bowl, add in the light brown sugar, corn syrup, shortening, beaten egg, pure vanilla and dash of salt. Stir well until smooth in consistency. Pour into the tart shells.
3. Place into the oven to bake for 10 to 15 minutes or until baked through.
4. Remove and cool for 20 minutes before serving.

Miniature Mac and Cheese Pies

If you thought miniature pies could only be sweet, these delicious pies will pleasantly surprise you. These are the perfect pies to prepare for those picky eaters in your home. **Makes:** 3 servings

Total Prep Time: 40 minutes

Ingredients:

- 2 Tbsp. of butter
- 2 Tbsp. of all-purpose flour
- 2 cups of whole milk
- 1 cup of grated Parmesan cheese
- Dash of salt and black pepper
- 7 ounces of macaroni pasta
- 3 ounces of pancetta, chopped
- 2 puff pastries, store-bought
- 3 slices of cheddar cheese
- 1 egg, beaten

Directions:

1. In a saucepan set over low to medium heat, add in the butter. Once melted, add in the all-purpose flour. Whisk until smooth in

consistency. Pour in the whole milk. Continue to whisk until smooth. Add in the grated Parmesan cheese. Season with a dash of salt and black pepper.

2. In a separate saucepan set over medium heat, add in the pancetta. Cook for 3 to 5 minutes or until crispy. Drain the excess grease. Set the pancetta aside.
3. In a pot set over medium to high heat, fill with salted water. Add in the macaroni. Cook for 8 to 10 minutes or until soft. Drain the pasta and set aside.
4. Preheat the oven to 350 degrees.
5. Cut out 3, 6 inch rounds from the puff pastry. Transfer into a greased miniature muffin pan, spreading along the bottom and sides evenly.
6. In a bowl, add in the cooked macaroni, Parmesan cheese mix and cooked pancetta. Stir well to mix. Pour over the crusts in the muffin pan. Top off with a slice of cheddar cheese. Top off with 3, 6 inch puff pastry rounds. Seal the edges.
7. Brush the tops of the pies with the beaten egg.
8. Place into the oven to bake for 30 minutes or until golden. Remove and cool for 5 minutes.
9. Serve.

Miniature Sweet Potato Pies

If you are looking for a delicious dessert dish to serve during your Thanksgiving holiday celebration, then this is the perfect dish for you to prepare.

 Makes: 24 servings

Total Prep Time: 30 minutes

Ingredients:

- ¾ pound of sweet potato, peeled and chopped
- 1, 9 inch pie crust
- ¾ cup of evaporated milk
- 2 egg whites
- ¼ cup of white sugar
- 2 Tbsp. of light brown sugar
- ¾ tsp. of powdered cinnamon
- 1/8 tsp. of powdered nutmeg
- 1/8 tsp. of powdered cloves
- ¼ cup of cranberries, cut into halves

Directions:

1. In a saucepan set over medium to high heat, add in the sweet potatoes. Cover with water. Allow to come to a boil. Cook for 5 minutes or until soft. Drain the potatoes and transfer into a bowl. Mash thoroughly until smooth in consistency.
2. Preheat the oven to 425 degrees.

3. Separate the pie crusts into 24 balls and press into a miniature muffin pan. Spread evenly along the bottom and sides to form tart shells. Set the shells aside.
4. In a food processor, add in the mashed sweet potatoes, evaporated milk, egg whites, light brown sugar white sugar, powdered cinnamon, powdered nutmeg and powdered cloves. Pulse on the highest setting until smooth in consistency.
5. Pour 1 tablespoon of this mix into each of the tart shells.
6. Place into the oven to bake for 10 minutes or until baked through. Remove and set aside to cool.
7. Garnish the top of the pieces with the cranberry halves.
8. Serve immediately.

Miniature Bourbon and Pecan Pies

These are the perfect pies to serve during the holiday season. They are incredibly sweet and packed with a crunchy deliciousness that is hard to resist.

Makes: 12 servings

Total Prep Time: 40 minutes

Ingredients:

- 12 miniature pie crusts
- 1 cup of pecans, chopped
- ½ cup of butter
- ¾ cup of light brown sugar
- ½ cup of light corn syrup
- 2 ounces of bourbon
- 1 tsp. of pure vanilla
- 3 eggs
- Dash of salt

Directions:

1. Preheat the oven to 350 degrees.
2. In a saucepan set over low to medium heat, add in the butter. Once melted, add in the light brown sugar and bourbon. Stir well until mixed. Remove from heat. Add in the corn syrup, pure vanilla and dash of salt. Stir well to mix.

3. In a bowl, add in the eggs. Whisk to beat. Pour in ½ cup of the hot liquid. Whisk the egg mix vigorously. Add into the saucepan and whisk to incorporate.
4. Place the miniature pie crusts onto a baking dish. Sprinkle the chopped pecans into the bottom of the pie crusts. Pour the filling over the pecans.
5. Set into the oven to bake for 15 to 20 minutes or until golden. Remove and set aside to cool for 10 minutes.
6. Serve immediately.

Miniature Cheddar and Broccoli Soup Pies

These pies may just be the best thing you have ever tried. One bite and I guarantee you will want to make these pies as often as possible.

Makes: 16 servings

Total Prep Time: 1 hour and 15 minutes

Ingredients:

- 2 Tbsp. of extra virgin olive oil
- 1 onion, chopped
- 1 clove of garlic, minced
- ¼ cup of all-purpose flour
- 1, 14 ounce can of coconut milk
- 4 cups of broccoli florets
- 1 to 2 cups of mushrooms, chopped
- 1 to 2 cups of chicken broth
- 1 tsp. of cayenne pepper
- ½ tsp. of powdered nutmeg
- ¼ tsp. of salt and black pepper
- 2 to 3 cups of sharp cheddar cheese, shredded and extra for topping
- 2 sheets of puff pastry
- 1 egg, beaten
- Dash of sea salt, for serving

Directions:

1. In a Dutch oven set over medium heat, add in the olive oil. Add in the chopped onion and minced garlic. Cook for 5 minutes or until soft. Add in the all-purpose flour. Whisk to mix. Cook for 3 to 4 minutes or until smooth in consistency.
2. Add in the chicken broth, broccoli florets, chopped mushrooms, cayenne pepper and powdered nutmeg. Season with a dash of salt and black pepper. Allow to come to a simmer. Lower the heat to medium. Cook for 15 to 20 minutes or until thick in consistency.
3. Pour half of the broccoli mix into a blender. Blend on the highest setting until smooth in consistency. Pour back into the Dutch oven. Stir well to incorporate.
4. Add in the cheddar cheese. Cook for 2 to 3 minutes or until melted. Continue to cook for 10 minutes or until thick in consistency.
5. Roll out the puff pastry on a flat surface. Cut out 4 ¼ inch circles from the dough. Place into a greased muffin pan, spreading along the bottom and sides. Pour the soup mix into the crust. Cover with 4 ¼ inch dough circles. Pinch the edges to seal.
6. Brush the tops of the pies with the beaten eggs. Season with a dash of sea salt.
7. Place into the oven to bake for 20 to 25 minutes or until golden. Remove and cool for 10 minutes before serving.

Miniature Canadian Butter Pies

These delicious pies are a classic Canadian delicacy that nobody will be able
to turn down. While it may take some time to prepare, it is well worth the
effort in the end.

Makes: 12 servings

Total Prep Time: 40 minutes

Ingredients:

- 2 cups of all-purpose flour
- 1 cup of shortening
- ½ tsp. of salt
- 5 Tbsp. of ice water
- 1 cup of light brown sugar
- 1 egg
- ½ Tbsp. of butter
- ½ tsp. of pure vanilla
- 1 Tbsp. of hot water
- ½ cup of coconut, flaked

- ½ cup of walnuts, chopped
- ½ cup of raisins

Directions:

1. In a bowl, add in the all-purpose flour and dash of salt. Add in the shortening and cut in until crumbly in consistency. Add in the ice water and stir well until a dough begins to form. Shape the dough into a ball. Cover and set into the fridge to chill for 15 minutes.
2. Place the dough in between two sheets of parchment paper. Roll into a rectangle. Slice out 12, 3 to 4 inch circles from the dough. Place into a greased muffin pan, spreading along the bottom and sides.
3. Preheat the oven to 350 degrees.
4. On a baking sheet, add the walnuts and flaked coconut. Place into the oven to roast for 5 to 10 minutes or until browned. Remove and set aside to cool. Increase the temperature of the oven to 450 degrees.
5. Fill the pie crusts with 10 raisins.
6. In a bowl, add in the white sugar, egg, soft butter, pure vanilla, hot water, roasted coconut and roasted walnuts. Stir well to mix. Pour into the pie crusts, filling each cup 2/3 of the way full.
7. Place into the oven to bake for 10 to 12 minutes or until golden. Remove and set aside to cool completely before serving.

Miniature Lemon Macaroon Pies

This is a delicious miniature pie recipe that is perfect to make during the hot summer months. It looks just as great as it tastes.

Makes: 24 servings

Total Prep Time: 40 minutes

Ingredients:

- 2 cups of coconut, sweetened and flaked
- ½ cup of white sugar
- 3/8 cup of all-purpose flour
- 1 tsp. of pure vanilla
- 2 egg whites
- 1, 3.4 ounce pack of instant lemon pudding mix
- 1, 8 ounce container of whipped topping
- 1 cup of coconut, sweetened and flaked

Directions:

1. Preheat the oven to 400 degrees. Grease a miniature muffin pan with cooking spray.
2. In a bowl, add in flaked coconut, white sugar, all-purpose flour, pure

vanilla and egg whites. Stir well until evenly mixed. Pour into the muffin cups.

3. Place into the oven to bake for 5 to 10 minutes or until the edges are browned. Remove and set aside to cool completely.
4. Prepare the lemon pudding mix according to the directions on the package. Pour into the pie shells.
5. Top off with the whipped topping and a sprinkling of ½ teaspoon of coconut.
6. Serve.

Miniature Breakfast Apple, Bacon and Cheddar Cheese Pies

This is a delicious pie recipe I know you will insist on prepare every morning for breakfast. While the size of these pies may be small, they are packed with a ton of flavor to make up for its small stature.

Makes: 6 servings

Total Prep Time: 35 minutes

Ingredients:

- ¾ pound of bacon, cooked and crumbled
- 1 cup of apple, peeled and chopped
- 1 cup of sharp cheddar cheese, shredded
- ½ cup of white onion, chopped
- 3 Tbsp. of sage leaves, chopped
- ½ tsp. of salt
- ½ cup of Bisquick
- ½ cup of whole milk
- 2 eggs

Directions:

1. Preheat the oven to 350 degrees. Grease a muffin pan with cooking spray.
2. In a bowl, add in the crumbled bacon, chopped apple, shredded sharp cheddar cheese, chopped white onion, chopped sage and dash of salt. Stir well to mix.
3. In a separate bowl, add in the Bisquick, whole milk and eggs. Whisk until smooth in consistency.
4. Pour 1 tablespoon of the Bisquick mix into the bottom of each greased muffin cup. Top off with ¼ cup of the bacon mix. Pour the remaining Bisquick mix over the top.
5. Place into the oven to bake for 25 to 30 minutes or until baked through. Remove and set onto a wire rack to cool for 10 minutes.
6. Serve.

Miniature Key Lime Pies

There is nothing that tastes better than homemade key lime pies. These miniature pies are so easy to make, I know you will want to make them every chance you get.

Makes: 12 servings

Total Prep Time: 1 hour and 25 minutes

Ingredients:

- 12 miniature graham cracker crusts
- 3 cups of sweetened condensed milk
- 1 cup of sour cream
- 1 cup of key lime juice
- 3 Tbsp. of grated key lime zest
- 2 key limes, thinly sliced
- 1, 7 ounce can of whipped cream

Directions:

1. Preheat the oven to 350 degrees.
2. Place the crusts onto a baking sheet.

3. In a bowl, add in the sweetened milk, sour cream, lime juice and
    grated lime zest. Stir well until smooth in consistency. Pour into
    the pie crusts.
4. Place into the oven to bake for 6 to 8 minutes. Remove and
    transfer into the fridge to chill for 1 hour.
5. Garnish the pies with a slice of the key limes and a topping of
    whipped cream.
6. Serve.

Miniature Shepherd's Pot Pies

If you are in a hurry to get dinner on the table, then this is one miniature pie recipe I know you will want to prepare. These pies are incredibly filling and packed with a flavor the entire family will love.

 Makes: 12 servings

Total Prep Time: 1 hour and 5 minutes

Ingredients:

- 1 box of Pillsbury pie crusts, soft
- ½ pound of lean ground beef
- 1 onion, chopped
- 4 tsp. of all-purpose flour
- ¾ cup of beef broth
- ½ tsp. of salt
- 1/8 tsp. of black pepper
- 1 ½ cups of mixed vegetables
- 1, 24 ounce pack of mashed potatoes

Directions:

1. Preheat the oven to 375 degrees.
2. Unroll the pie crusts onto a lightly floured surface. Cut out 6, 4 inch circles from the crust. Press the rounds into a greased muffin pan.
3. Place into the oven to bake for 10 to 12 minutes or until light brown.
4. In a skillet set over medium to high heat, add in the ground beef and chopped onion. Cook for 8 to 10 minutes or until the beef is browned. Drain the excess grease. Add in the all-purpose flour. Stir well until mixed. Add in the beef broth. Season with a dash of salt and black pepper. Cook for 2 to 3 minutes or until thick in consistency.
5. Add in the mixed vegetables. Stir well to incorporate.
6. Pour ¼ cup of the beef mix into the pie crusts.
7. Top off with the mashed potatoes.
8. Place back into the oven to bake for 20 to 25 minutes or until the mashed potatoes are browned.
9. Remove and cool for 10 minutes.
10. Serve.

Miniature Homemade Egg Pies

This is as simple as any pie gets. These Asian inspired miniature pies are perfect to make whenever you want to try something new.

Makes: 22 servings

Total Prep Time: 1 hour

Ingredients:

- 2 cups of all-purpose flour
- Dash of salt
- 10 Tbsp. of butter, chopped
- ¼ cup of powdered sugar
- 1 egg
- 2 Tbsp. of cold water
- 1 cup of water
- ¾ cup of white sugar
- 3 eggs
- 3/8 cup of evaporated milk
- ¼ tsp. of pure vanilla

Directions:

1. Preheat the oven to 400 degrees.
2. In a bowl, add in the all-purpose flour and dash of salt. Add in the chopped butter. Cut in until crumbly in consistency.
3. In a separate bowl, add in the egg and cold water. Whisk to mix. Add into the flour mix and stir well until a dough forms.
4. Wrap the dough in a sheet of plastic wrap. Set into the fridge to chill for 30 minutes.
5. Divide the dough in half. Roll out the dough halves until 1/8 inch in thickness. Slice out 22 rounds that are 3 ½ inch in thickness from the dough. Press into 2 inch tart pans.
6. In a saucepan over low heat, add in the remaining cup of water and white sugar. Stir well until the sugar dissolves. Remove from heat and set aside.
7. In a bowl, add in the eggs, milk and pure vanilla. Beat with an electric mixer until smooth in consistency. Add in the syrup mix and stir well to incorporate. Pour into the tart pans.
8. Place into the oven to bake for 20 minutes or until the crust is golden. Remove and set aside to cool for 15 minutes.
9. Serve.

Miniature Orange Mince Pies

This is a fresh tasting and sweet pie recipe that is perfect to make any day of the week. They are so easy to make, you can make them the moment you have a sweet tooth.

Makes: 18 servings

Total Prep Time: 40 minutes

Ingredients:

- 1 ¾ cups of all-purpose flour
- ¼ cup of powdered sugar
- 2 tsp. of powdered cinnamon
- 2/3 cup of butter, soft
- 2 Tbsp. of grated orange zest

- ¼ cup of ice water
- ¾ cup of mincemeat pie filling, prepared
- 1 egg, beaten
- ¼ cup of powdered sugar, for dusting

Directions

1. Preheat the oven to 400 degrees.
2. In a bowl, add in the all-purpose flour, ¼ cup of powdered sugar and powdered cinnamon. Stir well to mix. Add in the orange zest and ice water. Stir well until a dough forms.
3. Roll out the dough until ¼ inch in thickness. Cut out 18, 3 inch circles from the dough. Transfer into greased tart pans.
4. Fill the crusts with 1 tablespoon of the mincemeat pie filling. Top off with the remaining dough circles. Pinch the edges together to seal.
5. Brush the tops of the pie with the beaten egg.
6. Place into the oven to bake for 15 to 20 minutes or until the tops of the pies are golden. Remove and cool for 30 minutes.
7. Dust the tops of the pies with the remaining ¼ cup of powdered sugar.
8. Serve.

Conclusion

Well, there you have it! Hopefully by the end of this cookbook, you have found plenty of new and delicious miniature pie recipes that you can prepare from within the comfort of your own home. By the end of this cookbook, not only do I hope you have found plenty of pie dishes that you can make regardless of the occasion, but I also hope you have gained the confidence to try new dishes that you have never tried before. So, what is next for you? The next step for you to take is to begin making all of these delicious pie recipes for yourself. Once you have done that, don't hesitate to try making your very own miniature pie dishes completely from scratch. Good luck!